D0898175

ON LINE

# Artists in Profile

# ABSTRACT EXPRESSIONISTS

Rachel Barnes

Heinemann Library
Chicago, Illinois

Customer Service  888-454-2279

Visit our website at www.heinemannlibrary.com

Designed
Printed

07 06 05 04 03
10 9 8 7 6 5 4 3 2 1

**Library of Congress Cataloging-in-Publication Data**

Barnes, Rachel.
  Abstract expressionists / Rachel Barnes.
    p. cm. -- (Artists in profile)
  Includes bibliographical references and index.
  Summary: Discusses the characteristics of the Abstract Expressionism
  movement which began in the 1950s and presents biographies of thirteen
  Abstract Expressionist artists.
  ISBN 1-58810-644-6
  1. Abstract expressionism--New York (State)--New York--Juvenile
  literature. 2.  New York school of art--Juvenile literature. 3.
  Painting, American--New York (State)--New York--20th century--Juvenile
  literature. 4.  Painters--United States--Biography--Juvenile
  literature.
  [1. Abstract expressionism. 2. New York school of art. 3. Artists.]  I.
  Title. II. Series.
    ND212.5.A25 B37 2002
    759.13'09'045--dc21

                      2001005031

Originated by Ambassador Litho Ltd
Printed and bound in China by South China Printing Company

**Acknowledgments**

The author and publishers are grateful to the following for permission to reproduce copyright material: p. 5 Geoffrey Clements/Corbis; p. 6 Galleria Nazionale d'Arte Moderna, Rome, Italy/Bridgeman Art Library/ARS, N.Y. and DACS, London 2002; pp. 9, 47 Private Collection/Bridgeman Art Library/Kate Rothko Prizel and Christopher Rothko/DACS 2002; p. 11 Ernst Haas/Hulton; p. 12 Detroit Institute of Arts, USA/Bridgeman Art Library; p. 14 Gjon Mili/Rex, p. 16 Fritz Goro/Rex, p. 37 Martha Holmes/Rex/Timepix, p. 46 Ben Martin/Rex, p. 51 Nina Leen/Rex/Timepix; p. 15 Tate, London 2002/ADAGP, Paris and DACS, London 2002; pp. 17, 34, 44, 55 Tate, London 2002/ARS,N.Y. and DACS, London 2002; p. 19 National Portrait Gallery, Smithsonian Institution/Art Resource, N.Y.; p. 21 AKG; p. 22 Carnegie Museum of Art, Pittsburg U.S./AKG/Willem de Kooning Revocable Trust/ARS, N.Y. and DACS, London 2002; pp. 24, 25 Pollock Krasner Foudation, Inc./photograph courtesy Robert Miller Gallery, New York/ARS, N.Y. and DACS, London 2002; p. 27 Corbis/Colita; p. 28 Rheinisches Bildarchiv, Koln, Germany/Dedalus Foundation, Inc/VAGA, New York/DACS, London 2002; p. 29 Tate, London 2002/Dedalus Foundation, Inc./VAGA, New York/DACS, London 2002; p. 33 Ugo Mulas Estate, all rights reserved; p. 39 National Gallery of Art, Washington D.C./Bridgeman Art Library/ARS, N.Y. and DACS, London 2002; p. 40 Australian National Gallery, Canberra/Bridgeman Art Library/ARS, N.Y. and DACS, London 2002; p. 43 Hulton; p. 48 Burstein Collection/Corbis /Kate Rothko Prizel and Christopher Rothko/DACS 2002; p. 53 Peggy Guggenheim Foundation, Venice/Bridgeman Art Library.

Cover photograph: *Eyes in the Heat* by Jackson Pollock (1946). This image is reproduced with permission of the Bridgeman Art Library/Peggy Guggenheim Foundation.

**Author dedication**
The author would like to dedicate this book to Amy and Alice.

Some words are shown in bold **like this.** You can find out what they mean by looking in the glossary.

# Contents

9/2003
I $28.50

# What Is Abstract Expressionism?

Abstract Expressionism is the name for an artistic movement that grew in the United States in the 1940s and 1950s. It is also known as the **New York School,** since most of the movement's important artists lived there, at least for a time. During World War II, many influential artists had fled the fighting and persecution in Europe and ended up in New York. The Abstract Expressionist group was made up of artists who had either come from Europe or who were directly influenced by the movement's styles and techniques.

Abstract Expressionism is a term used for art that uses elements of **Expressionism** in an **abstract** way. Expressionist artists used bold colors and lines to express strong feeling and emotion. Abstract art is different from **figurative** or realist art, where the artist tries to recreate the appearance of actual objects or people. Abstract artists reduce things from the real world to basic shapes and forms, or create new forms from their imaginations. Abstract Expressionists were also influenced by **Surrealism.** The Surrealists tried to express the **subconscious** by using symbolic and dreamlike images. The Abstract Expressionists expressed things through the actual process of painting. The physical properties of paint (what it was like) were what was important.

Before the Abstract Expressionists, many American artists did not value American art as much as European art. Some American painters simply copied European styles. Others, called **American Scene Painters,** painted realist images of life in the rural and urban United States. The recognition of the Abstract Expressionists meant that for the first time the United States became known as an important force in **avant-garde** art. The term *avant-garde* is often used in art to describe anything radically new or different. While the Abstract Expressionists were influenced by European art, they created something that was entirely new. They began to create trends rather than follow them.

## Who were they?

The New York School was not, in the strictest sense, an artistic movement. The Abstract Expressionists included artists who had each developed their own individual styles. But there were enough similarities in the way they thought about and approached painting that they gradually became known as a group.

Jackson Pollock, Willem de Kooning, Helen Frankenthaler, Lee Krasner, and Franz Kline all became recognized for a technique called "action painting." This was where spontaneous physical movement and gestures were used to produce paintings. Jackson Pollock became most famous for his "drip" paintings, in which he dripped, poured, or squirted paint directly onto his canvases.

Other artists who fall under the title of Abstract Expressionists created different-looking work. These include Mark Rothko, Barnett Newman, and Clyfford Still. Their paintings are characterized by large areas, or "fields," of color. There is often no frame or edge to the painting, and the expanse of color covers the whole picture surface. This technique became known as "color field" painting.

*Men Playing Basketball,* by Elaine de Kooning
*Although the title of this work refers specifically to a group of athletes, the brushstrokes used by the artist communicate a feeling of dynamic movement, rather than actually describing the players.*

5

Both the "action" and "color field" painters shared methods and ideals. Paint is applied in bold, simple brushstrokes; dribbles, or splashes, and blocks of color are used to make the maximum visual impact. The huge physical size of the paintings matched the artists' grand philosophical ideas.

Abstract Expressionists all shared a philosophy that art was a search for individual or universal truth. The artists tried to find a way of painting that did not have to follow any particular style or **school** of art. This way, people would not associate the painting with anything else. They would just look at it as a painting and form their own ideas of what it meant. To understand the artists' radical and experimental approach to painting, you need to know something about the times they lived through.

## The Great Depression
The Wall Street Crash in New York is often seen as the starting point of the Great Depression. Wall Street is the **stock exchange** center for the United

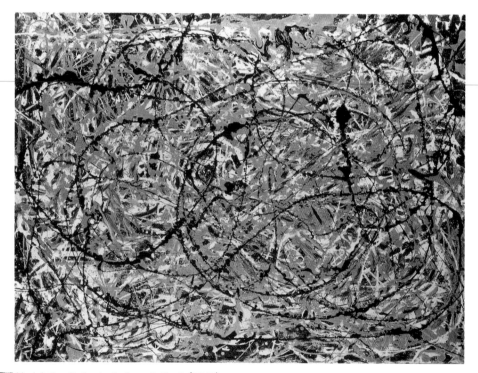

■■■ *Undulating Paths, by Jackson Pollock (1947)*
*Made in the year Pollock invented drip painting, this work expresses the feeling of wildness and freedom and the overwhelming sense of the paint's texture, which the artist was able to achieve with his new method of working.*

States. In October 1929, the stock market collapsed. The value of companies and the stock that people had bought in those companies as an investment, suddenly became nearly worthless. People panicked and tried to sell off vast numbers of shares. This made the problem even worse. The U.S. economy slumped, ending the financially well-off years of the 1920s. Businesses collapsed, and thousands were made penniless virtually overnight.

The Depression was felt all over the world, especially by countries relying on U.S. loans. In 1929, the United States stopped lending money abroad, and by 1930 nearly 2,000 banks collapsed as people rushed to withdraw their savings. Three years later there were over twelve million people unemployed in the United States.

## Federal Art Project

As the Depression deepened, the U.S. government started the Works Progress Administration (WPA) to create jobs for the unemployed. In 1934, it set up the Public Works of Art Project and started to book struggling artists to create **murals** to decorate public buildings. The WPA started up the Federal Art Project (FAP) in 1935. The FAP began to **commission** artists to do **easel paintings** and sculptures as well as murals. Most of the art made for the WPA was realist and featured images from daily rural or industrial life. The artists who specialized in this type of art were called **American Scene Painters.**

Participating artists were paid around 23 dollars a week—just enough to survive. More than a hundred community art centers were opened across the country, employing around 6,000 artists—almost three-quarters were living in New York. The FAP also created a sense of community, especially in Greenwich Village in New York. Artists such as Jackson Pollock, Willem de Kooning, Lee Krasner, and Mark Rothko were all involved. In fact, those who did not qualify because of their income, such as Barnett Newman, felt like they were missing out. Newman said, "I paid a severe price for not being on the Project with the other guys; in their eyes I wasn't a painter; I didn't have the label."

## World War II

World War II (1939–1945) was fought across much of Europe and Asia and had an even more profound effect on the civilian population than World War I (1914–1918). Technology had advanced since World War I—aircraft and tanks were used far more. Advances in bombing technology meant that towns and cities were more likely to be bombed. People were evacuated to safer areas, families were broken up, and countries were occupied by the enemy. Shortages of food and clothing were also commonplace. Many people who were able to fled Europe, fearing the advancing threat of Nazi Germany.

New York during World War II was full of artists who had fled Europe. Key members of the **Surrealists,** such as Salvador Dalí and Max Ernst, and other great **abstract** and **Cubist** artists, such as Fernand Léger, Piet Mondrain, and Marc Chagall, spent the war years in New York. These artists were the **avant-garde** of Europe, and many Abstract Expressionists looked to them for inspiration. Soon New York, rather than Paris, was established as the center of modern art.

European artists found life in New York different from life in Paris. The cafés of Paris provided places for artists to meet and discuss their work. However, there was no such tradition in New York. Art galleries like the Museum of Modern Art and the Julien Levy Gallery began to take the place of the café as artists' meeting places. However, it was the private gallery of Peggy Guggenheim that was the most important. Peggy Guggenheim came from a wealthy family that supported the arts, and she was an important art dealer. She was also married to the Surrealist artist Max Ernst. Her New York gallery, Art of This Century, was a key place for the Abstract Expressionists to exhibit in the 1950s.

## Surrealism

The Surrealists, who were the most important group of artists in Paris before World War II, had a major impact on Abstract Expressionist painters. The Surrealists were fascinated with the workings of the **subconscious** mind and the writings of the pioneer psychoanalysts Sigmund Freud and Carl Jung. They painted distorted, dreamlike images that represented the subconscious. Mark Rothko's early work was strongly dependent on Surrealist concepts and ideals, especially those of Joan Miró. She used abstract signs and symbols to express basic themes of life.

## Post–World War II United States

The **New York School** became an important force in the art world during the late 1940s, partly because Europe was still caught up in the aftermath of World War II. A good deal of European artistic creativity had been put on hold with so many artists called to fight, but significant art was being made at this stage in Europe. Much of it was in response to the events of the war and, in particular, the Holocaust—the attempted extermination of the Jewish people by Nazi Germany.

The United States, of course, also played a major role in the fight against Germany. The crucial difference was that the actual fighting did not take place on U.S. soil. Consequently, while Europe suffered a period of economic depression, the United States was about to enter a time of relative wealth.

## Reaction to world events

Abstract Expressionism was a response to a variety of factors, including earlier art movements and the political and social circumstances of the United States in the 1930s and 1940s. The horrors of World War II led some Abstract Expressionists to create abstract, rather than **figurative,** art. They felt their art should not represent the corrupt material world of their experience.

*Untitled,* by Mark Rothko (1953)
*The three-tiered effect of Rothko's color fields has sometimes been seen as expressive of the concept of the earth, heaven, and hell. Using abstract color with no frames, Rothko wanted to express feelings through color alone.*

# Helen Frankenthaler (1928– )

- Born December 12, 1928, in New York, New York
- Has lived in New York, Connecticut, and Vermont

## Key works
*Mountains and Sea*, 1952
*Before the Caves*, 1958
*The Other Side of the Moon*, 1995

Helen Frankenthaler, one of the youngest members of the **New York School,** invented an original, highly expressive form of Abstract Expressionism. She used vivid, luminous colors and rejected paintbrushes in favor of her own technique of soaking the canvas with paint.

Born on December 12, 1928, in New York City to Martha Lowenstein and Alfred Frankenthaler, Helen Frankenthaler had two older sisters, Marjorie and Gloria. Her background was cultured and middle class; her father was a New York State Supreme Court Justice, although he died when Helen was only twelve years old.

She first attended Brearleys, an exclusive New York girls' school, before moving to the more liberal Dalton School. At Dalton, she became the favorite pupil of the celebrated Mexican **mural** artist Rufino Tamayo. She later said he liked her because she painted just like him. "I used his **medium** literally; a third turpentine, a third linseed oil, and a third varnish," she recalls. Tamayo was the first professional artist she had ever met, and from the start she was fascinated with his singleminded approach to his work. She said later that he helped her realize what a serious and hardworking commitment it took to become an artist. He also taught her "practical methods and materials; how to stretch a canvas with neat corners, how to apply the brush."

While studying with Tamayo, she visited the old Guggenheim Museum on 72nd Street, which was near her family's apartment and Tamayo's gallery, Valentine. This was an important early exposure to advanced European art. As a teenager she also often went to exhibitions at the Museum of Modern Art with her sister Marjorie. On these outings she began to learn how to look at art, to analyze and to understand the elements of each work. She retained a vivid memory of Salvador Dali's *Persistence of Memory,* his famous **Surrealist** painting of a melted watch.

Frankenthaler stayed in New York for a semester after she graduated from Dalton, continuing to study with Tamayo. In the spring of 1946, she left for Vermont to attend Bennington College. Paul Feeley, the head of the art department, became a strong influence on her work. When she left school three years later, she went to Europe, traveling to Amsterdam, London, Zurich, Brussels, and Paris.

On her return to New York in 1949, she met the painters Lee Krasner, Jackson Pollock, and Elaine and Willem de Kooning. She also met the influential art critic Clement Greenberg, who was one of the greatest supporters of Abstract Expressionism. Over the next few years, she began to show her work at venues such as the Jewish Museum and the Whitney Museum of American Art.

*Frankenthaler was inspired by Jackson Pollock's invention of drip painting and, as this photograph of her at work confirms, used similar methods herself.*

For the following five years, she and Greenberg spent a great deal of time together. They attended exhibitions, analyzed paintings, and went to galleries, museums, and the regular Friday-night meetings of the Artist's Club. Often, they took trips to the country to paint from nature. Frankenthaler used these trips to explore a **representational** style and method of painting. She got rid of most of this representational work, but many of her later abstract paintings show a similar interest in the landscape tradition.

In 1951, Frankenthaler saw Jackson Pollock's exhibition at the Betty Parsons Gallery. His drip paintings, invented four years previously, changed the course of her art. Frankenthaler and Greenberg visited Pollock and his wife, Lee Krasner, at their home in East Hampton, New York, the following spring. There Frankenthaler saw Pollock's paintings and began to appreciate how he worked. Instead of using an easel, he laid his canvas right on the floor and then painted straight down from all sides. He abandoned the traditional brushes and oils in favor of enamel paint and a variety of dripping instruments. Frankenthaler noticed that in some places on Pollock's paintings, the paint had soaked directly into the canvas. In most traditional paintings, the paint does not soak in because the artist first uses a primer to seal the canvas and create a smooth

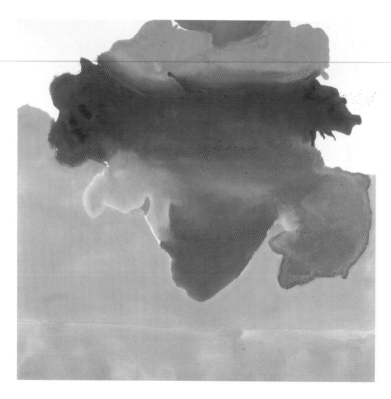

*The Bay,* by Helen Frankenthaler (1963)
*Initially influenced by Mark Rothko's color fields, Frankenthaler delighted in using bright colors to suggest the beauty and magic of the natural world.*

surface on which to paint. Frankenthaler experimented with staining canvases with paint, and in 1952 she created her early masterpiece using this technique called *Mountains and Sea*. In this work, she poured, rubbed, and dripped paint to form veils of soft colors that were absorbed into the fabric of the canvas.

In 1958, Frankenthaler married the painter Robert Motherwell. They traveled throughout France and Spain for several months on their honeymoon. However, the marriage was not destined to last. (Motherwell had been married twice before and would marry again after his twelve-year marriage to Frankenthaler.) But during the early years, they were very happy. Both artists benefited from the encouragement and support they gave to each other.

Initially the marriage might have impeded Frankenthaler's wider recognition as an artist. Motherwell was one of the major voices of Abstract Expressionism. Yet by her 40s, Frankenthaler's own individual, poetic response to Abstract Expressionism was increasingly seen as a force in its own right. As fellow painter Morris Louis said, Frankenthaler was "a bridge between Pollock and what was possible." In 1969, a huge **retrospective** exhibition—a show covering her entire career—at the Whitney Museum confirmed this. Throughout the 1960s and 1970s, she taught at universities such as Yale, Princeton, and Bennington College. Today, she remains active as a printmaker.

## Morris Louis (1912–1962)

Morris Louis (born Louis Bernstein) was born in 1912 in Baltimore, Maryland. He first studied painting at the Maryland Institute of Art (1927–1932) then worked under the WPA easel painting project (1937–1940). Louis's work was initially influenced by the sharp lines and **geometric** forms of **Cubism.** Later he became influenced by Abstract Expressionism. This was particularly so after 1952, when he was introduced to Jackson Pollock's "drip" paintings. Most important, however, was a meeting with Helen Frankenthaler, who taught him to pour acrylic paint directly onto the canvas without using brushes. His work bought together the moods and scenes of the soft, evocative, painterly **Impressionism** of Claude Monet with Abstract Expressionism. Like Monet, however, he was frequently dissatisfied with his work and went through periods of destroying much of it. Louis died in Washington, D.C., in 1962.

# Arshile Gorky (1904–1948)

- Born April 15, 1904, in Khorkom, Turkish Armenia
- Died July 21, 1948, in Sherman, Connecticut

**Key works**

*Some in Khorkom*, 1936
*Waterfall*, 1943
*One Year the Milkweed*, 1944

Arshile Gorky was born Vosdanig Adoian on April 15, 1904, in Turkish Armenia. His father deserted the family in 1908, running away to the United States in order to avoid serving in the Turkish army. During World War I, there were terrible massacres in Armenia and the rest of Gorky's family fled the country in 1915. They were in desperate poverty, so bad that Gorky's mother died of starvation in March 1919. Following her death, Gorky and his sisters joined a refugee ship and crossed to the United States to join their father.

▮▮ *Gorky was well aware of his good looks and loved to dress in flamboyant clothes. But his extroverted nature concealed a darker side that became more pronounced as he got older.*

By the time Gorky arrived in the United States, he knew he wanted to be an artist. He studied at Boston's New School of Design before leaving for New York at the age of 21. There he studied and later taught at the Grand Central School of Art. It was at this point he decided to change his name. He chose "Arshile" as a variant on the name of a legendary mythical hero Achilles. The name "Gorky" in Russian means "the bitter one."

From the start, Gorky dressed the part of the artist, in flamboyant clothes to set off his handsome, romantic looks. He explored many different artistic styles in his early years as a painter. Initially he favored the works of the artist Paul Cézanne before becoming, like many other artists of this time, completely obsessed with the **Cubist** Pablo Picasso. Gorky was so talented at imitating other artists that for a long time he was not recognized as a serious artist in his own right. One of his works from this time, *The Artist and His Mother* (c. 1929–1934), is based on an old family photograph and shows the influence of Cézanne. It also indicates that Gorky continued to be haunted by memories from his difficult childhood.

For a while during the **Great Depression,** Gorky was too poor to buy paints and canvas. But he was determined to continue with his art at all costs. In 1930, he was included in a show at the Museum of Modern Art—Forty-Six Painters and Sculptors Under Thirty-Five. In 1934, he had his first one-man show at the Mellon Gallery in Philadelphia. In 1935, he married Marny George. Unfortunately, it was not long before they separated.

By the mid-1930s, Gorky was developing his own highly individual style. He was moving away from **geometric** shapes influenced by Cubism and began to use sweeping, **organic** shapes. A little later he met André Breton, the leader of the **Surrealist** group of writers and painters. Breton agreed to write the catalog preface for Gorky's show at the Julian Levy Gallery in New York. At the beginning of the 1940s, Gorky got married again, this time to Agnes Magruder.

Gorky was at last a success in the art world. However, his happiness was not to last. On January 26, 1946, a fire raged through his studio and destroyed about

30 paintings. Then, in February 1946, he had to have an operation for cancer. On top of all this, in December 1947, his father died. Gorky became emotionally unstable. In addition, he and his wife, Agnes, suffered marital problems. Agnes, worn out by Gorky's jealousy, left him. In June 1948, he was injured in a bad car crash, breaking his neck and paralysing his arm so that he was unable to paint.

It was the combination of all these misfortunes that caused Gorky to take his own life on July 21, 1948, a month after the crash. It was just at the time that his art, for which he had struggled for so long, was becoming widely recognized.

*Waterfall,* by Arshile Gorky (1943)
*Gorky's style of painting, like his personality, was emotional. Waterfall wonderfully evokes the sensation of cascading water.*

# Franz Kline (1910–1962)

- Born May 23, 1910, in Wilkes-Barre, Pennsylvania
- Died May 13, 1962, in New York, New York

### Key works
*Siskind*, 1958
*Black Iris*, 1961

Franz Rowe Kline was born in Wilkes-Barre, Pennsylvania, on May 23, 1910. He was the second child of four. Neither of his parents was originally from the United States. His father came from Hamburg, Germany, and his mother was English. When Kline was just seven years old, his father committed suicide. The emotional scars were to haunt him throughout his life. In 1919, two years after his father's death, the nine-year-old Kline was sent to an institution for fatherless children, Girard College in Philadelphia, where he stayed for six years. Kline was unhappy there and was finally removed by his mother in 1925. He joined his mother, sister, brother, and new stepfather in the coal mining town of Lehighton in eastern Pennsylvania. The sooty industrial landscape would influence his art for years to come.

*This famous photograph of Kline was taken in the last decade of his life when he was at last beginning to receive recognition. He sits in his studio, surrounded by his dramatic black–and–white paintings.*

When Kline was in high school, he had an accident in football practice. It was during his recovery that he started to draw seriously. In 1931, he went to Boston University and afterwards to the Boston Art Students League. In 1935, he went to England. His mother was English, and he had always been fascinated by all things English. He enrolled at the conservative Heatherley's School of Fine Art in London.

Kline met a young dancer named Elizabeth Vincent Parsons at Heatherley's. She was a ballet dancer in the Sadler's Wells ballet and modeled at the art school. In 1938, Kline returned to New York, where he would spend the rest of his life, and Elizabeth followed him. They got married and were initially happy together.

However, Elizabeth suffered from schizophrenia, a mental illness. Her health was probably not helped by their poverty. They were so poor that they found it almost impossible to keep up with rent payments. Three times they were evicted from apartments, and there was never any stability to their home life. In 1948, Elizabeth's condition deteriorated, and she entered a mental hospital in New Jersey, where she would remain for the next twelve years.

During his first years as an artist, Kline had worked in a **representational** style. He had favored drawing things from real life and making realistic illustrations. However, in the 1950s, Kline began to express himself in a new way. Kline had his first one-man show at the Egan Gallery in 1950. Here, he showed his new **abstract** style. His large, striking images, made up of bold, straight brushstrokes that had the appearance of Chinese calligraphy—the art of decorative writing—were very well received. Kline had discovered his new method almost by accident—by projecting a small drawing onto a wall to create the effect of enlarged microscopic detail. This resulting style was to characterize the rest of his work.

*Meryon*, by Franz Kline (1960–1961)
*This work is typical of Kline's love of using huge black brushstrokes on a white background.*

# Elaine de Kooning (1918–1989)

- Born March 12, 1918, in Brooklyn, Pennsylvania
- Died February 1, 1989, in Southhampton, New York

**Key works**

*Self-Portrait*, 1946
*Baseball Players*, 1953
*Jardin du Luxembourg VII*, 1977

Elaine Marie Fried was born on March 12, 1918, to an Irish Catholic mother and a German Protestant father. Her intelligent, eccentric mother was a strong influence on Elaine, providing a good role model of an independent woman. She grew up to be precocious, competitive, and outgoing. When asked about her artistic talent, de Kooning said, "I never made a decision about being a painter. When I was five, I made drawings like all children."

De Kooning regularly visited New York's Metropolitan Museum of Art to see the great European masters. As soon as she graduated from high school she entered Hunter College in New York. She dropped out the following year because she wanted to become a painter. "I just couldn't stand not having a paint brush in my hand," she said. "I didn't feel that I had time for college. I knew what I wanted to do."

She entered the Leonardo da Vinci School in New York City, where she later remembered: "I drew all day every day." She also worked as a model for other artists, to help pay her tuition fees. She was still a student when she first met Willem de Kooning. From the first time they met in 1938, they fell instantly in love. A mutual friend recalled: "[Willem] seemed interested in her in a way that he had never been interested in any of the other women around him. He . . . didn't want any other woman." At this time she worked in a number of styles, creating "action painting" abstractions as well as **figurative** compositions.

Elaine and Willem's marriage, which took place in 1943, was to last—on and off—for almost 50 years, although they spent as long apart as they were together. They only separated in the mid-1950s. But before she left him, de Kooning had helped establish Willem as an artist, neglecting her own art in the process. She had become well known as an art critic, however. She wrote extensively on post–World War II American art for the important magazine *Art News*. Her relationship with Willem had been destructive, though. By the time she left him, both had mental problems.

After they separated, de Kooning was able to focus on her own art and develop her own talents as a painter. A lot of her art focused on men. During the 1950s, she often painted sports stars, such as basketball players and bullfighters, to express her interest in movement. She even traveled from the years 1950 to 1953 with the New York Yankees and the Baltimore Orioles, painting works that convey the quick motions of the game of baseball, such as *Baseball Players*, in 1953.

De Kooning supported herself by working as a visiting professor at universities across the United States. In 1978, she heard that Willem was ill, and she returned to New York to look after him. Under her guidance his career became revitalized.

Although it was de Kooning who had returned to take care of her husband, it was her health that collapsed first. She died in 1989 from lung cancer.

■■ *Self-Portrait*, by Elaine de Kooning (1946)
*Elaine de Kooning was extremely conscious of her beauty and shows it to good advantage in this self-portrait.*

# Willem de Kooning (1904–1997)

- Born April 24, 1904, in Rotterdam, the Netherlands
- Died March 19, 1997, in East Hampton, New York

## Key works
*Excavation*, 1950
*Woman I*, 1950–1952
*The Visit*, 1966

Willem de Kooning, along with Mark Rothko and Jackson Pollock, was one of the great Abstract Expressionists. Like them, he was powerfully inventive, developing a unique and personal approach to painting. But like them he also had a darker, self-destructive side.

He was born on April 24, 1904, in Rotterdam in the Netherlands. When he was only three years old, his parents divorced. He was left in the care of his mother, who appears to have abused him mentally and possibly physically.

When he was twelve years old, he was apprenticed to a local firm of commercial artists and decorators. He also went to night classes at the Rotterdam Academy of Fine Arts and Techniques, where he studied until 1924. Many of the Dutch art students he met there idolized the work of the artist Piet Mondrian. Mondrian painted in an **abstract** style, with sharp black lines filled with bright blocks of color. He wanted to reduce elements of the world around him into their simplest forms. That way, anyone could understand his paintings in a basic, spiritual way.

As he grew up, de Kooning became dissatisfied with life in Rotterdam and began to long for adventure. In 1926, at the age of 22, he made one of the biggest decisions of his life. He stowed away on a ship and went to the United States. When de Kooning arrived, he found work in New Jersey as a house painter. He was pleased with the money he could earn—nine dollars a day was quite a large salary. He stuck at this for about five months and then decided to look for work doing illustration and applied artwork. He worked on a portfolio of examples of his work. He was hired quickly and expected to earn a much higher salary for this skilled work than for housepainting. It was a shock, therefore, when he received his pay at the end of the first two weeks. He said, "the man gave me 25 dollars, and I was so astonished that I asked him if that was a day's pay. He said, 'No, that's for the whole week.' And I immediately quit and went back to housepainting."

So ended his first exploration of the art world. In 1927, he packed up and left New Jersey and ended up in New York. Again he found work in commercial art, painting signs and working on displays for shops.

He did not completely abandon his art, though. In New York, de Kooning made an important friendship with the artist Arshile Gorky. He shared a studio with him for some time. De Kooning was still working as a house and sign painter, which helped him develop painting techniques that he taught Gorky. But he also felt that he learned a lot from Gorky's **intuitive** approach to art: "Gorky didn't have [training] . . . and for some mysterious reason he knew more about painting and art—he just knew it by nature—though I was supposed to know and feel and understand, he really did it better."

De Kooning never lost his Dutch accent and was known in his younger days in New York as "the handsome Dutchman."

■■ *Woman VI*, by Willem de Kooning (1953)
*This energetic, dynamic image of a woman was part of a series exploring movement.*

During the **Great Depression,** de Kooning struggled to make ends meet. Like many fellow artists, he went to work on the Federal Art Project. Unfortunately, in 1936, the government banned immigrants from the project, especially those like de Kooning who had come to the United States illegally.

Yet, despite the struggle, he was gradually becoming better known. In 1940, he was asked to design the sets and costumes for a production of the ballet *Les Nuages* for the Ballets Russes de Monte Carlo.

In 1938, de Kooning met Elaine Fried, whom he would later marry in 1943. Elaine was beautiful, energetic, and a tremendous support to her husband. She did a great deal to promote his work and was partially responsible for his recognition as one the great Abstract Expressionists. However, after a difficult marriage, they separated in the mid-1950s.

De Kooning worked on a number of different themes at the same time. He created purely **abstract** works as well as **figurative** images. In 1951, his painting *Excavation*—a purely abstract work made up of slashes of black and white paint—won the prestigious Logan Medal and Purchase Prize. It was recognized as one of the most important pieces in the development of Abstract Expressionist art. At the same time, de Kooning was working on a series of **Expressionist** female paintings, such as *Woman I.* Many people found these paintings menacing and shocking; they were not the images of female beauty traditionally associated with the subject.

Although his lifestyle were becoming increasingly uncontrolled, de Kooning was by 1960 becoming famous. In 1968, a huge **retrospective** exhibition was held at the Stedelijk Museum in Amsterdam. This was his first return to the Netherlands since leaving penniless at age 22. During the 1960s and 1970s, de Kooning experimented with different types of art, including sculpture and printmaking.

Elaine returned in 1978. In 1980, de Kooning entered a phase of great artistic creativity. From 1981 to 1990, he finished more than 300 paintings. In 1989, he was diagnosed with Alzheimer's, a progressive disease that eventually decays memory and damages other mental functions. Elaine died that year from lung cancer. De Kooning lived almost another decade, suffering increasingly from his illness. He died March 19, 1997, on Long Island. In 1999, the journal *Art News* recognized de Kooning as one of the 25 most influential artists of the 1900s.

# Lee Krasner (1908–1984)

- Born October 27, 1908, in New York, New York
- Died June 19, 1984, in New York

**Key works**

*Solstice* (series), 1949
*Primeval Resurgence*, 1961
*Right Bird Left*, 1965

*Self-Portrait*, by Lee Krasner (1931–33)
*Krasner was a highly independent artist in her own right, yet she had to fight to have this acknowledged after she married Jackson Pollock.*

Lee Krasner was born Lena Krassner in Brooklyn, New York, on October 27, 1908. Her family were Russian-Jewish immigrants who had only just arrived in the United States. Krasner went to school in Brooklyn, then transferred to the only public high school in New York that taught art to girls, Washington Irving. She studied at the Cooper Union, the Art Students League, and the National Academy of Design. She modeled and waitressed to earn money until 1934, when she was employed by the Public Works of Art Project. In 1937, she returned to her art studies, this time with the artist and important teacher Hans Hofmann.

Krasner studied and read about art constantly. By 1939, well before many of the other Abstract Expressionists, she had already developed her own personal painting style, influenced by **Cubism**. In 1941, she was invited to participate in an important exhibition for the design firm of McMillen Inc., where Jackson Pollock's work was also being shown. They had met only once before, at a party in 1936, but Krasner decided to visit him in his studio. The relationship blossomed during the following year.

Krasner devoted much of her energy to helping promote Pollock's work, and she was one of the main reasons for his success. She helped him stage his first one-man show at Peggy Guggenheim's gallery, Art of This Century. She aided him in his ongoing health problems. The couple moved out of New York City to the comparative tranquility of nearby Long Island in 1945. They married shortly after.

For much of her early marriage, Krasner's own art was overshadowed by her husband's. She continued to work, though. She constantly redefined her painting style and sometimes repainted or destroyed her earlier works. In 1955, the Stable Gallery in Manhattan showed a group of her **collage** paintings. The exhibition helped to reestablish her as one of the most important **abstract** painters of her time.

In Pollock's last desperate years, when he found it increasingly hard to paint, it is probable he felt undermined by Krasner's growing success as an artist. Their relationship was very strained at the time he died in a car crash in 1956. In 1957–1959, she worked on a series called *Earth Green*, which has been seen as a response to her grief and anger over her husband's death. Around this time, the **feminist movement** took up her cause and she responded, demonstrating in protest about the Museum of Modern Art's neglect of female artists.

Krasner's work from the 1960s and 1970s reflected an interest in natural imagery. She also further experimented with collage. Exhibitions such as the 1965 **retrospective** of her work at the Whitechapel Gallery in London helped establish her as an important figure in the Abstract Expressionist movement. In 1983, the Houston Museum of Fine Arts opened a full retrospective of her work, which traveled throughout the United States. Krasner died in the summer of 1984, before the show reached New York.

*Untitled*, by Lee Krasner (1949)
*Krasner was a committed abstract painter from early in her career. Her work often reveals a love of pattern for its own sake.*

# Robert Motherwell (1915–1991)

- Born January 24, 1915, in Aberdeen, Washington
- Died July 16, 1991, in Provincetown, Massachusetts

## Key works
*Pancho Villa, Dead and Alive,* 1943
*Elegy to the Spanish Republic,* 1953–1954
*Je t'aime* (series), 1955–1958

Robert Motherwell was a key member of the Abstract Expressionist group. Unlike most of the Abstract Expressionists, he had a highly privileged upbringing. While others were struggling to make a living during the **Depression,** Motherwell was touring Europe. One of the most intellectual of the Abstract Expressionist artists, he was a writer and seriously studied theories and ideas about art. He was also a talented printmaker and **draftsman.**

Robert Burns Motherwell was born on January 4, 1915, in Aberdeen, Washington. His parents were Scottish and Irish. His father, a conservative man, worked as chairman of a bank and wanted his son to go into law or business. Motherwell seemed destined for something else, though. He was talented from an early age—when he was just eleven years old he received a scholarship to study art.

When Motherwell was a teenager, his family moved to San Francisco. Soon after, he was sent to Moran Preparatory School in central California, where he first looked at modern art in the *Encyclopedia Britannica.* Later, he wrote about the reasons he was moved to the new school:

> I went to a prep school in California, because I lived in San Francisco and as a teenager developed horrible asthma. San Francisco is foggy and damp. . . . A specialist at Berkeley advised my father that the San Francisco climate was murder, so I got sent to this new little prep school halfway between San Francisco and Los Angeles. The air is very dry, twelve miles from the ocean, with oak trees and no underbrush, very dry soil, marvellous climate. . . . [A]ll the students there were all emotionally disturbed; the parents were getting divorced or whatever, and essentially it was a school to park battered children.

■■■ *Motherwell, photographed in later years, when he was enjoying huge fame and considerable wealth as one of the most important Abstract Expressionists.*

In 1932, Motherwell went to Stanford University, where he studied philosophy. It was there that he experienced modern art in person for the first time. At a party he saw some paintings by the French **Expressionist** artist Henri Matisse that he said "went through [him] like an arrow." Matisse was interested in how colors and shapes could be used to express emotions and sensations. He wanted to convey not how things looked but how he felt about the things he painted. Matisse influenced many painters in the 1900s, including some Abstract Expressionists.

After Motherwell graduated from Stanford, he studied philosophy as a graduate student at Harvard University between 1937 and 1938. After this, he went on a trip around Europe with his father and sister. This was an important experience for him. It was his first exposure to European literature and artists, which would exert a major influence on his art. The trip also gave Motherwell a great taste for traveling in Europe, something he would do whenever the opportunity arose in later life.

*Elegy to the Spanish Republic (Basque Elegy)*, by Robert Motherwell (1967)
*Motherwell's brand of Abstract Expressionism often dealt with politics. This bold and powerful image is symbolic of a lost era of Spanish history.*

Motherwell decided after this trip that he wanted to be a painter, not go back to his studies at Harvard. His father was disappointed. Motherwell moved to New York, where he studied from 1940 to 1941 with the important artist and writer Meyer Schapiro. Through him he met the **Surrealist** artists living in New York, notably Roberto Matta Echaurren, who became an important friend. He traveled with Matta to Mexico, where he spent four months painting and absorbing the colors of Mexican folk art. On his trip, Motherwell met a young Mexican actress, Maria Emilia Ferreira y Moyers, who would soon become the first of his four wives.

Under the influence of the Surrealists, Motherwell explored **automatism,** or spontaneous drawing used to bring forth images from the artist's **subconscious** mind. Many of the Abstract Expressionists used automatism as a way to get in touch with their intuition, to base their art in instinct and emotion rather than logic and reason. As Motherwell wrote, "The emergence of abstract art is one sign that there are still men able to assert feeling in the world. Men who know how to respect and follow their inner feelings, no matter how irrational or absurd they may first appear."

Back in New York, his career as an artist was quickly taking off. He had moved away from **figurative** art, that is, art with a subject like a person or object. He began to paint in an **abstract** way, often just making a patchwork of brilliant colors, lines, and marks. He abandoned the planning stages and started each painting with no set ideas. Many of Motherwell's works from this time reflect the harsh atmosphere of World War II. He made rough-looking **collages** of torn paper stained with dark paint. In 1944, he had his first one-man show at Peggy Guggenheim's gallery, Art of This Century. In 1945, he signed a contract with the dealer Samuel Kootz, which would last for the next ten years.

It was at this time Motherwell met the other Abstract Expressionists, Barnett Newman and Mark Rothko, who was to become a lifelong friend. During the summer, Motherwell taught art classes at Black Mountain College in North Carolina, and in the winter he lived on Long Island.

After a couple of years, his wife Maria complained that she felt isolated on Long Island, so in 1948 they moved back to New York City. But the marriage was by now failing, and they divorced the following year. That same year Motherwell met Betty Little in Reno, Nevada. They soon married and eventually had two daughters, Jeannie and Lise.

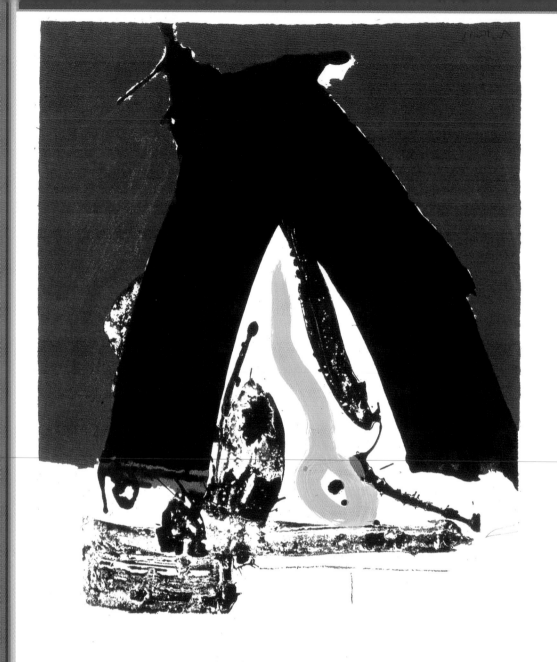

*Untitled D*, by Robert Motherwell (1970)
*In 1970, Motherwell said: "Most people ignorantly suppose that artists are the decorators of our human existence. . . But actually what an artist is, is a person skilled in expressing human feeling." Abstract Expressionists wanted to get away from the realism that had so far dominated American art.*

It was also at this time that Motherwell began his friendship with the important sculptor David Smith. He mourned him deeply when he was killed in a car accident a few years later.

Motherwell is probably best known for his abstract paintings from this time on the theme of the Spanish Civil War, such as *Elegy to the Spanish Republic*. The war started in 1936, when rebels revolted against the democratically elected government. It ended in 1939, with the victory of the rebels, who had received support from Nazi Germany. Motherwell and many others were saddened for many years by this blow to democracy.

In the late 1950s, there were a number of changes in Motherwell's personal life. He and Betty were divorced. He made a series of small paintings called *Je t'aime* (French for "I love you") in 1955–1958 that expressed his feelings about the failure of their marriage. Motherwell soon met the painter Helen Frankenthaler, though, and they wed in 1958. This relationship was to last much longer and be far more fruitful than his earlier marriages. They immediately went to Europe for their honeymoon, and they stayed to paint for several months in the south of France.

Motherwell continued to experiment with new styles and themes. In the 1960s, for instance, he made works inspired by the ocean around Provincetown, Massachusetts, where he spent summers. He tried to apply paint to his canvases in a way similar to the spray of waves.

Motherwell was now internationally acknowledged as one of the major forces of the **New York School;** honors were heaped upon him in the last two decades of his life up until his death in July 1991. He had **retrospectives**—exhibitions that covered his whole career—in São Paulo, Brazil (1961); Pasadena, California (1962); New York (1965); Mexico City (1968); and Barcelona and Madrid, Spain (1980). In 1982, the Bavarian Museum of Modern Art opened a room devoted to his works.

His marriage to Helen Frankenthaler ended in 1971, but in the year of his divorce he met the photographer Renate Ponsold, whom he wed the following year. They remained happily married until Motherwell's death in July 16, 1991, after a series of operations on his heart.

# Barnett Newman (1905–1970)

- Born January 29, 1905, in New York, New York
- Died July 4, 1970, in New York

### Key works
*Onement I*, 1948
*Vir heroicus sublimis*, 1950–1951
*Stations of the Cross* (series), 1958–1966

Barnett Newman was associated with the Abstract Expressionists, although at first appearance his work seems different. While artists like Jackson Pollock or Franz Kline developed the ideas for their paintings while working on them, Newman carefully planned each work before even lifting a brush. His extraordinarily simple canvases have more in common with Mark Rothko's work. They are painted in large blocks of color with sharp defining lines through or across them. His techniques paved the way for the next major New York movement—**Minimalism.** Unlike the Minimalists, however, Newman was ultimately interested in the spiritual quality of his paintings.

Born in Manhattan in 1905 into a Polish-Jewish family, Newman was the oldest of four children. His father, Abraham, had built up a successful clothing manufacturing company in New York, after arriving as a penniless immigrant. The family lived a good life in the suburbs of the Bronx, thanks to his father's profitable business. Newman attended public school and Hebrew school. He later remembered his childhood as happy.

He became fascinated by art as a teenager and would skip school just to spend entire days at the Metropolitan Museum of Art. At the age of seventeen, he persuaded his parents to let him enroll at the Art Students League while finishing his last year of high school. He continued to study at the Art Students League while attending the City College of New York from 1923 to 1927.

Newman hoped to pursue art as a career, but his father had other plans for him—to carry on the family business. Newman and his father made a deal. They agreed that he would work with his father for two years, and at the end of it, if he could retire with $100,000, he could take the money and follow his own dreams. But the Wall Street Crash of 1929 changed everything for Newman.

Although his father refused to sell the business off, it was in desperate trouble. For the next ten years, Newman struggled alongside his father to save the failing company. At the same time he brought in extra money by teaching art to high school students. Although this must have been deeply frustrating for someone with the ambition to become a painter, he later denied feeling bitter about it. He claimed that a lot of his experience had actually taught him valuable artistic principles. He had learned about "the meaning of form, the visual and tactile nature of things; how to take a rag and make it come to life. I learned the difference between a form and shape."

■■■ *Newman had to wait much longer than his fellow Abstract Expressionists to achieve the recognition he deserved for his unique contribution to the movement.*

In 1936, he met and married a young teacher named Annalee Greenhouse. Their first meeting was not promising. Newman loved to debate, and the two of them had a fight about the merits of the composers Mozart and Wagner that ended with Annalee storming out! It was to be a solid marriage, however. Annalee was a staunch supporter throughout the years that followed.

Not long after his marriage, Newman destroyed much of his early, **representational** artwork and stopped painting. He thought that the way he had been painting seemed unimportant compared to the seriousness and horror of World War II. Though he did not paint for five years, Newman thought and wrote about art. He also threw himself enthusiastically into studying botany (plant life), geology (rocks), and ornithology (birds).

*Adam*, by Barnett Newman (1951–1952)
*This is a famous example of Newman's zip paintings, where a strong vertical line breaks into the color. It took Newman many years to find his own way of responding to Abstract Expressionism.*

For many artists such a sustained period of inactivity might spell the end, but not for Newman. In 1944, he began to create art again; he worked on a series of drawings based around seeds and patterns of growth. Soon after this he rented a studio close to Willem de Kooning. His important break as an artist came with his painting *Onement I* in 1948.

With *Onement I* and the paintings that followed, he developed an innovative way of working. He would mask off areas of his canvas with tape. By painting over the tape and then removing it, Newman was able to get perfectly straight and sharp lines, which he referred to as zips. His works from this period all contain the zips. Over time he played with different edges, colors, numbers, and widths, but the zip was there in one form or another. Some people have interpreted the zips as abstractions of human forms. Newman was more interested in them simply as a visual element in his paintings, in which he sought to create an overall sense of harmony and wonder.

Meanwhile Newman was also active as an art critic and **curator,** helping to promote the reputation of fellow Abstract Expressionists. His loyal support of the group made it particularly painful for Newman when his own first one-man show in 1950 at Betty Parsons Gallery was severely criticized by other artists. His show consisted of paintings like or inspired by *Onement I*, with its orange zip painted on a red-brown background. The controlled simplicity of Newman's paintings appeared at odds with the expressive emotionalism of work from the other Abstract Expressionists. Newman, however, always claimed that there was an emotional or spiritual content in his art.

Newman's financial problems continued after the disaster of his first two one-man shows, and he toyed with the idea of giving up painting. He did however have one important supporter. The influential critic Clement Greenberg felt that a show that had caused so many artists to react so violently, even if they did not like the work, must have some value.

It was not until the late 1950s that Newman's paintings began to make a major breakthrough. In 1958, four of his paintings were included in the Museum of Modern Art's show *The New American Painting.* His rapidly spreading reputation was secured with the exhibition Stations of the Cross at the Guggenheim Museum in 1966. Newman died on July 4, 1970, in New York.

# Jackson Pollock (1912–1956)

- Born January 28, 1912, in Cody, Wyoming
- Died August 11, 1956, in East Hampton, New York

## Key works
*Naked Man with a Knife*, 1938
*Alchemy*, 1947
*Number 1, 1950 (Lavender Mist)*, 1950
*Blue Poles II*, 1952

Jackson Pollock was arguably the most important pioneer of Abstract Expressionism and one of the most revolutionary painters of the 1900s. He abandoned the tradition of **easel painting,** executing his works on canvas spread on the floor.

Paul Jackson Pollock was born on January 28, 1912, at Watkus Ranch in Cody, Wyoming. His mother, Stella May, and father, Le Roy, both of Scottish-Irish descent, were born and raised in Tingley, Iowa. Jackson was their youngest son, and he had four older brothers. They were named Charles, Marvin, Frank, and Sanford.

While Pollock was still a baby, the family moved to California and later to Arizona. For the next few years, there would be constant moves between the two states as his father struggled to make ends meet. When Pollock was nine years old, his father left home altogether, leaving Stella to struggle with her five unruly boys. She was not strong with disciplining them. Her youngest son developed a wild side to his character and was often in trouble at school.

In 1922, Pollock's oldest brother, Charles, enrolled at Otis Art Institute in Los Angeles. He regularly sent home copies of the art magazine the *Dial*, which was Pollock's first exposure to modern art.

In 1926, Pollock graduated from Grant Elementary School in Riverside and enrolled at Riverside High School, where he joined the Reserve Officers' Training Corps (ROTC). Although Pollock was only fifteen years old, he was expelled from the ROTC because he hit a fellow student. He left Riverside High School the following spring and in the summer of 1928 the family, still without his father Le Roy, moved to Los Angeles. Pollock enrolled at the Manual Arts High School where he concentrated on art, but in March 1929 he was expelled for disciplinary problems. In September 1929, he was allowed

The photographer Hans Namuth took a series of now-famous films and photographs of Pollock in action, dripping and squirting the paint onto his canvas laid down on the floor of his studio.

back but was soon expelled again. These were difficult and painful years for Pollock, who as yet had found no positive direction. Trying to deal with his feelings of insecurity and unhappiness was difficult for him.

At the age of eighteen, Pollock joined his brother Charles in New York with the intention of becoming an artist. At the New York Art Students League he was taught by the **American Scene Painter** Thomas Hart Benton. Pollock was at first strongly influenced by his work, although he later said "My work with Benton was important as something against which to react very strongly." Benton had tried to come up with a uniquely American way of painting, and his subject matter was often drawn from the country's early frontier history. Some of Pollock's earliest works, such as *Going West* (1934–1935), show the influence of Benton. The young Pollock was also attracted by Benton's tough image—perhaps not the best role model for a young man who already had problems of his own.

Over the next ten years, Pollock would live on the brink of extreme poverty as he took a series of jobs, including lumberjack and janitor, to sustain his life as an artist. In 1938, the strain became intolerable: he suffered a major nervous breakdown from which he did not recover for six months. With his brother Sanford's encouragement, he began psychiatric treatment for alcoholism under a **psychoanalyst.** The themes he was introduced to in his treatment— such as the belief in the **subconscious** mind as the root of all creativity— would greatly influence Pollock's approach to painting. Many of his paintings seem to reflect an inner search for some deep, spiritual, or unconscious meaning behind life.

In 1941, Pollock met the artist Lee Krasner. They would not marry for another four years, but Krasner was to become an invaluable supporter. She introduced him to many of the Abstract Expressionists and exposed him further to **Cubism** and **Surrealism.** Pollock's big professional breakthrough, however, came in 1942, when he met the influential art dealer, Peggy Guggenheim. She started to show Pollock's work in her gallery, called Art of This Century. In 1944, some of his paintings were published in the intellectual magazine the *Nation.* His talent was spotted by the art critic Clement Greenberg, who hailed Pollock as the author of "some of the strongest paintings I have yet seen by an American."

From this time on, he began to receive more recognition, not all of it favorable. His paintings from this time were quite large, some of them eight feet wide, with **abstract** forms and symbols scrawled on the surface. He often named his works after he finished them, giving them titles from literature or mythology.

Pollock invented his drip paintings around 1947, soon after he and Krasner had moved to Long Island. Working on the floor, he developed a way of painting in which he poured, dripped, or splashed the paint onto the canvas, allowing gravity to play a part in how the work turned out. Walking around the painting, at times standing on it, Pollock became immersed in the act of painting. He was obsessed with idea of leaving a record of himself in his work and incorporated handprints, footprints, ashes, and other personal artifacts into his paintings.

In a statement that he made in 1947, Pollock described the process he used to make his art:

> My painting does not come from the easel. . . . On the floor I am more at ease. I feel nearer, more a part of the painting, since this way

■ ■ ■ *Lavender Mist: Number 1*, by Jackson Pollock (1950)
*This painting is one of the most celebrated of the drip style. The paint, in unusually gentle pastel shades, is densely layered to evoke wonderful sensations of a wild and profuse nature.*

I can walk around it, walk from the four sides and literally be in the painting.

Pollock's drip painting style was formed by a combination of earlier experiences and other influences. These included energetic Mexican **mural** paintings and Native American culture. When he was a child, Pollock had explored the ruins of Native American settlements. As he grew older, he became increasingly fascinated by the Hopi religious custom of making ritual sand paintings on the floor.

The new style of painting that Pollock had created was also influenced by the Surrealist idea of **automatism,** a spontaneous way of creating art. Pollock used automatism to release the power of his subconscious mind. At the same time, Pollock was a great admirer of Cubism and Cubist artists such as Pablo Picasso. Although Pollock's paintings may appear wild and uncontrolled, he actually organized many of his works around the Cubist grid in order to give the paintings structure.

In the last four years of his life, Pollock became increasingly depressed. This was the point that his wife, Lee Krasner's, own career was just taking off. He reworked existing paintings, yet clearly he was suffering from artist's block. He had invented drip painting and revolutionized twentieth-century art, but having done so he seemed unable to do anything else.

III *Blue Poles II*, by Jackson Pollock (1952)
*Pollock first became famous in 1949 when an issue of* Life *magazine asked, "Is he the greatest living painter in the United States?" Twenty years after he created* Blue Poles, *one of his most famous paintings, it was bought for two million dollars by the Australian government.*

By the spring of 1956, Pollock had not painted for eighteen months. He felt uncomfortable with how critics were interpreting his work. He struggled with the idea that Abstract Expressionism was not supposed to have a particular subject. Pollock was always aiming to achieve this, to get as far from **figurative** painting as possible. But now felt he had failed to do so.

## Hans Hofmann (1880–1966)

Hans Hofmann was born in Bavaria, Germany, in 1880. As a young man he trained as an engineer but in the late 1890s he decided he wanted to study art. From 1904 to 1914 he spent most of his time in Paris, where he met the great artists Henri Matisse, Pablo Picasso, Georges Braque, and Paul Delaunay. He opened his own art school in Munich in 1915.

He settled in New York in 1932 and taught first at the Art Students League and then, starting in 1933, at his own school. He instructed a whole generation of artists, including some of the Abstract Expressionists, about the latest in European art.

Hofmann did not exhibit his own paintings until 1944 because he was afraid his students would imitate him rather than find their own styles. His works were **abstract** compositions based on nature and characterized by brilliant and expressive color. He made many of his greatest paintings in the last fifteen years of his life.

He died in New York on February 17, 1966.

In an interview with art historian Selden Rodman, he admitted that art always, to a greater or lesser degree, had to have some sort of subject.

On August, 11, 1956, Pollock was killed in car crash late at night. Although Pollock had never managed to earn more than a meager living from his art, by the time he died he had become an almost mythic figure in the art world.

# Ad Reinhardt (1913–1967)

- Born December 24, 1913, in Buffalo, New York
- Died August 30, 1967, in New York, New York

## Key works
*Abstract Painting,* 1959
*Abstract Painting,* 1960–1966
*Black Painting (Series),* 1963

Ad Reinhardt belonged to the generation of the Abstract Expressionists, but he has been called the godfather of **Minimalism**. He was deeply critical of many of the artists in New York who he thought painted wholly for the sake of making money. He held the firm belief that "art is art" and "everything else is everything else," and the two should not be confused. He meant that artists who claimed that their work had some deep significance and power for life or death (like some of the Abstract Expressionists) were frauds and worthy of contempt. Yet even though he was highly critical of them, his artistic style owed a lot to the Abstract Expressionists.

Ad Reinhardt was born Adolph Dietrich Friedrich Reinhardt in Buffalo, New York, on Christmas Eve 1913. His parents were both immigrants, his father Russian and his mother German. Reinhardt's interest in art was even noticeable as a small child. He showed a flair for painting and entered and won a competition when only seven years old. Later, he won a prize for a pencil portrait of the boxer Jack Dempsey.

When he was 22 years old he went to Columbia University in New York and was taught by the famous art historian Meyer Schapiro. Reinhardt was interested in politics, writing, and painting in his student days and became the editor of the campus magazine *Jester.* He did not become serious about art until he was in his mid-twenties, when he quickly got involved with **avant-garde** artists in New York. He left Columbia and managed to get a place on a public art project funded by the Federal Art Project (FAP). He discovered that the only form of art he was really attracted to was **abstract:** "I was born for it and it was born for me," he said. Through the FAP he met other artists and eventually joined a group whose style he was drawn to, the American Abstract Artists (AAA). The AAA group had almost all the abstract artists in the country in it, totaling about 40 or 50.

■ *Reinhardt in a late photograph of him with one of his* Black Paintings.

The FAP supported Reinhardt until he got a job working as a journalist for the newspaper *PM* in 1941. The United States joined World War II in 1942 after the bombing of Pearl Harbor in Hawaii by the Japanese. Reinhardt was drafted to serve as a sailor in the navy and forced to leave the newspaper. The military "didn't know what to do with me, so they made a sort of photographer out of me . . . I was always thrown in with a bunch of kids. I was 29 then. I was called Pop. I was the old man of every outfit."

*Abstract Painting No. 5*, by Ad Reinhardt (1962)
*Reinhardt described these black canvases as "the first paintings that cannot be misunderstood."*

Reinhardt was discharged from the navy in 1945 and returned to the *PM* newspaper. Not long after his return, he was fired. But soon after that, he found a teaching post at Brooklyn College. He taught for the rest of his career. He never really rated himself as a very good teacher. During this time he was increasingly vocal about his opinions of the art world. He made satirical sketches that poked fun at his peers and generally criticized the art world. But he still harbored dreams of becoming an artist himself. Most of his art from the 1940s was gestural and **abstract** like that of other Abstract Expressionists.

His breakthrough came in 1946 with his first one-man show at the Betty Parsons Gallery. Over the next decade, people began to invest in his work, and he achieved commercial success. This was something that he had never sought for himself and had always disliked intensely in others. To him it seemed unworthy and degrading to sell or exploit talent for money.

In 1953, he began to produce the paintings for which he is best known. He painted **monochrome** canvases in red, black, and blue, patterned with barely visible squares in different tones and shades of the same color. Seven years later, in the 1960s, all of his paintings became black, square, and uniform in size.

Reinhardt wanted his paintings to be free of symbolic, literary, or emotional associations. What he was trying to create was "a pure, abstract, non-objective, timeless, spaceless, changeless, relationless, disinterested painting ... ideal, transcendent, aware of nothing but Art." The subject of his paintings were the paintings themselves, a quality he shared with the **Minimalists.**

By the end of his life, Reinhardt was making enough money from his art to fulfill another of his dreams, to go traveling in the Far and Middle East. In 1958, he visited Japan, India, Iran, and Egypt, and in 1961, he traveled to Turkey, Syria, and Jordan.

In 1967, the Jewish Museum in New York held a **retrospective** exhibition of his work. Reinhardt had been an important member of the modern movement and was proud of that. He had been a part of both Abstract Expressionism and Minimalism. He claimed, half-jokingly, that he was, "the only painter who's been a member of every **avant-garde** movement in the last 30 years." Reinhardt died on August 30, 1967, in New York.

# Mark Rothko (1903–1970)

- Born September 25, 1903, in Dvinsk, Russia (now Dugavpils, Latvia)
- Died February 25, 1970, in New York

**Key works**
*Untitled,* 1949
*Red, Brown, and Black,* 1958
*Black on Maroon x 8 (The Seagram Murals),* 1959

Marcus Rothkovich was born into a Jewish family in the Latvian town of Dvinsk on September 25, 1903. Marcus had two older brothers and one older sister. Their father, Jakob Rothkovitch, was a pharmacist. The children's upbringing was strict and traditional. They grew up during a period when Jews were being persecuted in Russia. It was a time of political unrest and many people, including the government, unfairly blamed the Jews. Rothko remembered the fear and the threatening environment for the rest of his life.

▮▮ *Taken towards the end of his life, this photograph suggests the darker side of Rothko's nature, which despite huge fame and fortune would eventually overwhelm him.*

When Rothko was seven years old, his father emigrated to the United States with his two oldest sons. Three years later, the rest of the family joined them in Portland, Oregon. Only seven months after the rest of the family arrived, Rothko's father died, leaving the family very poor. Rothko said he remembered feeling permanently hungry as a child.

Unlike many of the Abstract Expressionists, Rothko did not dream in childhood or adolescence of becoming an artist. He was a very good student and won a scholarship to go to Yale University in 1921. At Yale he intended to be an engineer, but at age twenty, after only two years in college, he decided to drop out for a bit to "wander around, bum around, starve a bit."

He headed for New York, and a year later he enrolled at the Art Students League. In spite of two years of studying art there he would always describe himself as a self-taught artist. A few years later he took a teaching job at Central Academy in Brooklyn, a Jewish school attached to a synagogue—a Jewish house of worship—to help support his initially precarious life as a painter. He also worked part-time as an actor, took painting jobs backstage in theaters, and worked as an illustrator to supplement his income.

In 1932, Rothko married Edith Sacher, a jewelry designer. He also worked with many other Abstract Expressionists on the Federal Art Project. In 1935, he met Arshile Gorky and another member of the New York School, Adolph Gottlieb. With Gottlieb he formed a group called the Ten—a group of **Expressionists**, including Edith, who exhibited together over the next decade. In 1938, Rothko officially became a U.S. citizen. A couple of years after this, he began to use more the American-sounding name Mark Rothko, although he would only change it legally in 1959.

During World War II, Rothko's first marriage failed, and he met the woman who would become his second wife, Mary Alice Beistle, who was known as Mell. In 1944, his career as a painter was at last beginning to take off. By this time he had met other painters with similar ideas to his own, such as Jackson Pollock

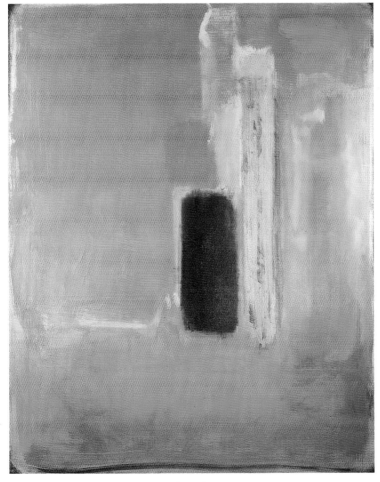

*Central Green,* by Mark Rothko (1949)
*Made the year that Rothko invented his color fields, the colors at this stage in his career were usually clear and luminous.*

and Willem de Kooning. Rothko's works from this time were heavily influenced by **Surrealism** and featured **organic** shapes. He wanted to express mythic themes using pure color and forms.

Rothko's first one-man show was at the famous art dealer Peggy Guggenheim's gallery in 1945. This was the breakthrough he had long dreamed of, although it was not for another ten years that his paintings sold for a lot of money.

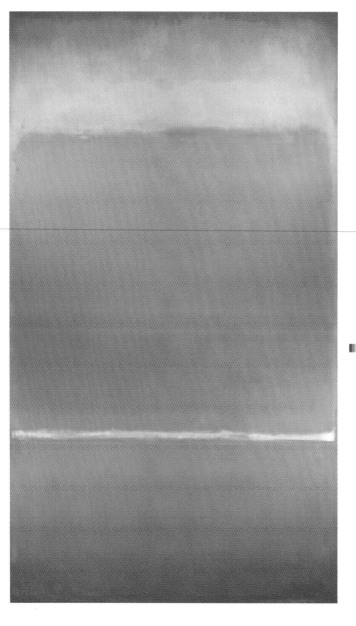

*Number 7*, by Mark Rothko (1951)
*In his works of this time, Rothko often paints his canvases in three tiers, sometimes interpreted as earth, heaven, and hell. It was Rothko himself who said that his paintings were about "tragedy, ecstasy, and doom."*

## Adolph Gottlieb (1903–1974)

Adolph Gottlieb was born in New York on March 14, 1903. He left high school in 1919 and joined the Art Students League. In 1935, Gottlieb and Rothko helped to establish an artists' group called the Ten, which was devoted to **Expressionist** and **abstract** painting. He used **automatism** to create improvisational and expressive paintings.

In 1970, Gottlieb suffered a stroke that paralyzed the left side of his body. However, he continued to paint from his wheelchair. Gottlieb died on March 4, 1974, in New York City.

By 1949, Rothko was beginning to paint in what would become his signature style. He created large paintings of shimmering color, allowing paint to soak into the canvas and form soft, radiant fields. He tried to express mood and emotion simply through the size and character of these color fields. He did not want the subject matter of conventional, **figurative** paintings to distract from the meaning of the painting. He saw his works as personal expressions of emotions and almost religious or spiritual feelings. He thought that he could make viewers have the same kind of spiritual experience just by looking at his paintings: "the fact that lots of people break down and cry when confronted with my pictures shows that I communicate with those basic [human] emotions. The people who weep before my pictures are having the same religious experience I had when I painted them."

Rothko was preoccupied with the idea that each painting relied on the viewer for its meaning or value. If the viewer was sensitive and took time to look at the painting properly then it would live. If a viewer was unsympathetic or not sensitive, then the painting would just appear to be meaningless and dead. He wanted to control the environments where his works were displayed. For instance, after he finished a group of paintings to decorate the Four Seasons restaurant in the Seagram Building in New York City, he decided that the location was bad. He withdrew from the **commission** and eventually gave the paintings to the Tate Gallery in London.

Rothko's first full-scale **retrospective** at the Museum of Modern Art in New York was followed by a one-man show at the Whitechapel Gallery in London. But achieving huge fame on both sides of the Atlantic did little to dispel the depressive, anxious side to his nature that had always been there. Some people interpret his increasingly dark and moody paintings from this period as reflections of his emotional state. His marriage to Mell finally broke under the strain. He spent the last wretched months of his life alone, living and working in his studio, before ending his life there on February 25, 1970, surrounded by his paintings.

# Clyfford Still (1904–1980)

- Born November 30, 1904, in Grandin, North Dakota
- Died June 23, 1980, in Baltimore, Maryland

**Key works**
*July-1945-R*, 1945
*Untitled*, 1961 1963 A, 1963
*1963-A*, 1963

Clyfford Still had grand ideas about art. For him his own brand of Abstract Expressionism was a life-and-death matter, which would in time bring him both critics and fans. Although his aims and style had much in common with other Abstract Expressionists, Still remained independent and was always seen as a bit of an outsider. Critics still question whether he should really be categorized as an Abstract Expressionist.

Still was born on November 30, 1904, in Grandin, North Dakota. His father, who was an accountant, moved the family to Spokane, Washington, the following year. When Still was six years old, the family began to spend more time in Alberta after the Canadian government opened the area to people who wanted to settle there. He loved his childhood in Canada and throughout his adult life would make frequent visits back there.

Still attended Edison Grammar School in Spokane, where he became especially interested in both art and music. After he had graduated, he took frequent trips to New York to the Metropolitan Museum of Art to see the original versions of paintings that he had "learned to love through the study of their reproductions." His enthusiasm for art led him to enroll at the Art Students League in New York, but he very quickly left, finding the teaching unimaginative and completely unhelpful.

In 1926, he went to Spokane University. However, he soon decided to drop out and go back to his family in Canada. In 1931, he returned to the university as a teacher. For the next ten years he would earn his living teaching at Spokane, and then, after 1933, at Washington State University in Pullman. Although he got along well with the students, he often found the staff unadventurous and unexciting, and their tried-and-trusted approach irritated him. Above all, Still sought a personal vision and wanted to free himself from the influence of **schools** of art before him.

At this time his art was mostly **figurative** and he worked on his style and technique by beginning to paint a series of **Expressionist** figure studies. He worked as a shipbuilder in California from 1941 to 1943 and then taught at Virginia's Richmond Professional Institute for two years. He continued to paint whenever he could, and his new works now grew into large abstract canvases made in thick **impasto.** These had much in common with the way Abstract Expressionism was developing in New York. The one-man show he was given at the San Francisco Museum in March 1943 was a breakthrough for him.

*Still sits third from the right in the back row, surrounded by fellow Abstract Expressionists including de Kooning, Newman, and Pollock.*

Soon afterwards, he met Mark Rothko for the first time while they were both teaching at a summer school at the University of California, Berkeley. This was to be an important relationship for both men, although from the beginning it was competitive. Rothko helped Still, introducing him to Peggy Guggenheim, who invited Still to exhibit some paintings in the Fall Salon at her gallery, Art of This Century. Later, in 1946, she gave him a one-man show. He was nervous about the response his paintings would get and made plans to leave New York to avoid the opening.

Still returned to Canada in 1947 to take up teaching again, and he built himself a small house there, virtually single-handedly. He did not cut himself off from New York completely and kept in contact with Rothko, who arranged to have some of Still's work shown. In spite of their friendship, there were some tension and rivalry between Rothko and Still. Rothko was always anxious to know what Still was up to, particularly to know how big his canvases were. Aware of this, Still once mischievously sent the message "I'm now doing paintings the size of postage stamps!" This, of course, was very far from the truth. Still was anxious to protect his own work, about which he had some grand ideas. He thought that by looking at his work people could find their way to mental and spiritual freedom. His paintings, with their jagged vertical forms, recall the shape of soaring mountains or the spires of Gothic cathedrals. They seem to reach toward the open spaces of the heavens.

By the late 1940s, Still was well established in California and his paintings were commanding increasingly high prices. He harbored dreams of establishing an artist-directed school with Rothko in New York, but Still was impatient and not willing to make compromises. Eventually, he got fed up with his colleagues and their inability to make decisions. The school did eventually open but without Still's involvement.

Still's strong independence had probably helped him steer clear of the self-destructive tendencies, such as depression, shared by other members of the Abstract Expressionist group. But it also had its down side. He became increasingly reluctant to show his paintings. He did however agree to stage a one-man show at the Albright-Knox Art Gallery in Buffalo, in 1959, which proved to be a triumph. Throughout the 1960s, he exhibited with the Marlborough-Gerson Gallery, and he became increasingly well known. He continued to believe that art was a force that could free people from social conformity. Unlike other members of the group, he lived to ripe old age. As a result, he lived to see his name honored as one of the great American painters of the century. Clyfford Still died on June 23, 1980, in Baltimore, Maryland.

■■ *Jamais,* by Clyfford Still (1944)
*Still always remained
aloof from other Abstract
Expressionists. This early
powerful, dynamic, and
totally abstract image
shows how instrumental
he was in forging a new
style in the early days
of the movement.*

# The Next Generation

The influence of Abstract Expressionism was not limited to New York. It also had an impact on a group of artists working in California, particularly those working with the teacher David Park at the California School of Fine Arts in San Francisco.

## Richard Diebenkorn (1922–1993)

Richard Diebenkorn was born in 1922 in Portland, Oregon. As a child he was always drawing. In 1940, he went to New York, where he first saw the work of Robert Motherwell, and during the mid–1940s he taught with Clyfford Still and Mark Rothko. Diebenkorn's works from the 1950s show the influence of the Abstract Expressionists, but he is most famous as a founder of the Bay Area **figurative** school in California. Diebenkorn died in 1993.

## Minimalism

The **Minimalists** reacted against the ideas of the Abstract Expressionists. Most of the Abstract Expressionists believed that art should have a spiritual quality. The Minimalists believed that the physical properties of a work of art were more important than spiritual ones. They thought that the clarity and simplicity of their works would make them easy to understand. Key artists involved in this movement included Carl Andre, Dan Flavin, Donald Judd, Robert Morris, and Frank Stella.

## Frank Stella (1936– )

Frank Stella was born in 1936 in Malden, Massachusetts. He studied painting at Phillips Academy in Andover, Massachusetts, before graduating from Princeton University with a history degree. He was inspired by the work of Ad Reinhardt. Between 1959 and 1961, Stella painted simple, **monochromatic** paintings that were typical of Minimalism. He used ordinary black house paint to create his canvases. Four of these works were shown in an exhibition called *Sixteen Americans* at the Museum of Modern Art in New York, along with the work of Ellsworth Kelly, Jasper Johns, and Robert Rauschenberg. Stella lives in New York and continues to paint.

## Ellsworth Kelly (1923– )

Ellsworth Kelly was born in Newburgh, New York, in 1923. He studied at the School of the Museum of Fine Arts in Boston from 1946 to 1947 before going to the famous École des Beaux-Arts in Paris. In France, Kelly discovered **Surrealism** and began to use **automatism** to create his works. He based his early geometric abstract paintings on architectural and natural forms.

In 1954, Kelly returned to New York, and in 1956, he had his first one-man exhibition there. Three years later his work was shown with Frank Stella's in the exhibition *Sixteen Americans*.

*Hyena Stomp*, by Frank Stella (1962)

*This painting was made with ordinary household paint. It is rigidly **geometric**, very unlike the expressive canvases of the Abstract Expressionists. Yet it is clear that the Minimalist painters, like Stella, were influenced by the movement as well as reacted against it.*

55

# Timeline

**1903**  Mark Rothko born September 25

**1904**  Arshile Gorky born April 15; Willem de Kooning born April 24; Clyfford Still born November 30

**1905**  Barnett Newman born January 29

**1908**  Lee Krasner born October 27

**1910**  Franz Kline born May 23

**1912**  Jackson Pollock born January 28

**1913**  Ad Reinhardt born December 24

**1914**  World War I begins

**1915**  Robert Motherwell born January 4

**1918**  World War I ends; Elaine (Fried) de Kooning born March 12

**1928**  Helen Frankenthaler born December 12

**1929** stock market crashes

**1934** U.S. Government sets up Public Works of Art Project

**1935** U.S. Government sets up Federal Art Project

**1936** International Surrealist exhibition in London

**1939** World War II begins

**1942** Peggy Guggenheim gallery, Art of This Century, opens in New York

**1943** Willem de Kooning and Elaine Fried marry

**1945** World War II ends; Jackson Pollock and Lee Krasner marry

**1947** Jackson Pollock invents drip painting

**1949** Mark Rothko invents color field

**1958** The New American Painting show at the Museum of Modern Art in New York; Robert Motherwell and Helen Frankenthaler marry

# Glossary

**abstract** removed from the recognizable. In terms of an art work it is not recognizable as an object, landscape, or person. A work where color and shape are more important than what they represent.

**American Scene Painters** artists active in the 1920s and 1930s who favored realistic scenes of daily life

**automatism** spontaneous drawing used to recreate images from the artist's subconscious mind

**avant-garde** pioneers or innovators in any sphere of the arts

**collage** piece of art made up of different materials, such as cuttings from newspapers, string, fabric, and paint

**commission** piece of work specifically requested by a group or art collector

**Cubism/Cubist** early twentieth-century school of painting and sculpture in which objects are shown as abstract geometric forms without realistic detail; often involving transparent cubes and cones

**curator** person who organizes and exhibitions or oversees art collections

**draftsman** person who draws plans or designs

**easel painting** making a painting with the canvas on a wooden structure (easel)

**Expressionism/Expressionist** art in which traditional ideas are abandoned in favor of a style that exaggerates feelings or expressions

**feminist movement** movement that emerged in the 1960s to fight for equal rights for women

**figurative** art in which recognizable figures or objects are portrayed

**geometric** from geometry, which is the study in mathematics of the angles and shapes formed by the relationship of lines, surfaces, and solids in space

**Great Depression** time of economic depression that lasted several years. It began in the United States in 1929 when the stock markets crashed.

**impasto**  paint applied in thick or heavy lumps that brings texture to a work

**Impressionism**  movement started in France in the 1860s by Claude Monet and Pierre Renoir. It was a revolutionary; paintings were completed in just a few hours, as opposed to months, and brush strokes were broken up with a new emphasis on the texture of the paint.

**intuitive**  using knowledge or sensations gained through personal insight rather than rational thought

**medium**  substance that an artist uses to create a work

**Minimalism/Minimalist**  style of art developed in New York in the 1960s using a minimum of line and color

**monochrome**  painting done in different shades of the same color

**mural**  painting made directly onto a wall, usually in a public space

**New York School**  another term for the Abstract Expressionist movement

**organic**  characterized by forms derived from objects in nature such as flowers

**political activism**  taking part in political activities

**psychoanalyst**  person trained to treat patients suffering from anxieties and nervous disorders. Psychoanalysis was developed by Sigmund Freud.

**representational**  art depicting recognizable things in the real world

**retrospective**  exhibition of an artist's work from beginning to end

**school**  group of artists working in a similar way during a particular time

**stock exchange**  place where shares in different businesses are bought and sold. A share is part-ownership of a business.

**subconscious**  hidden level of the mind and the thoughts that go on there

**Surrealism/Surrealist**  movement originally developed in Paris in 1921 that aimed to express the subconscious mind by the use of bizarre, irrational, absurd, and dreamlike images

# Resources

## List of famous works

**Helen Frankenthaler (1928– )**
*Mountains and Sea*, 1952, private collection, on loan to National Gallery
     of Art, Washington, D.C.
*Before the Caves*, 1958, National Museum of Women in the Arts,
     Washington, D.C.

**Arshile Gorky (1904–1948)**
*Some in Khorkom*, 1936, private collection
*Waterfall*, 1943, Tate Modern, London, England
*One Year the Milkweed*, 1944, National Gallery of Art, Washington, D.C.

**Franz Kline (1910–1962)**
*Painting No. 7*, 1952, Guggenheim Museum, New York
*Siskind*, 1958, Detroit Institute of Arts, Michigan
*Black Iris*, 1961, Museum of Contemporary Art, Los Angeles, CA

**Elaine de Kooning (1918–1989)**
*Self-Portrait*, 1946, National Portrait Gallery, Washington, D.C.
*Baseball Players*, 1953, Telfair Museum of Art, Savannah, GA
*Sunday Afternoon*, 1957, Ciba-Gelgy Corp., New York
*Jardin du Luxembourg VII*, 1977, National Museum of Women in the Arts,
     Washington, D.C.

**Willem de Kooning (1904–1997)**
*Evacuation*, 1950, The Art Institute of Chicago, Illinois
*Woman I*, 1950–1952, Museum of Modern Art, New York
*The Visit*, 1966, Tate Modern, London, England

**Lee Krasner (1908–1984)**
*Primeval Resurgence*, 1961, Museum of Contemporary Art, Los Angeles, CA
*Right Bird Left*, 1965, Ball State University Museum of Art, Muncie, IN

**Robert Motherwell (1915–1991)**
*Pancho Villa, Dead and Alive*, 1943, Museum of Modern Art, New York
*Elegy to the Spanish Republic #34*, 1953–1954, Albright-Knox Art Gallery,
     Buffalo, NY

**Barnett Newman (1905–1970)**
*Onement I*, 1948, Tate Modern, London, England
*Vir heroicus sublimus*, 1950–1951, Museum of Modern Art, New York
*Stations of the Cross* (series), 1958–1966, National Gallery of Art,
      Washington, D.C.

**Jackson Pollock (1912–1956)**
*Naked Man with a Knife*, 1938, Tate Modern, London, England
*Alchemy*, 1947, Guggenheim Museum, New York
*Number 1 (Lavender Mist)*, 1950, National Gallery of Art
      Washington, D.C.

**Ad Reinhardt (1913–1967)**
*Abstract Painting*, 1959, Marlborough International Fine Art, London, England
*Abstract Painting*, 1960–1966, Guggenheim Museum, New York
*Black Painting* (series), 1963, Tate Modern, London, England

**Mark Rothko (1903–1970)**
*Untitled*, 1949, Metropolitan Mueum of Art, New York
*Red, Brown, and Black*, 1958, Museum of Modern Art, New York
*Black on Maroon x 8 (The Seagram Murals)*, 1959, Tate Modern, London,
      England

**Clyfford Still (1904–80)**
*July-1945-R*, 1945, Albright-Knox Art Gallery, Buffalo, NY
*Untitled*, 1961, National Gallery of Art, Washington, D.C.
*1963-A*, 1963, Albright-Knox Art Gallery, Buffalo, NY

# Where to see Abstract Expressionist art

## The Museum of Modern Art
11 West 53 Street
New York, NY 10019
(212) 708-9400
www.moma.org
Work by many of the Abstract Expressionists artists, including Kline, de Kooning, Motherwell, and Newman, is permanently on display.

## Guggenheim Museum
1071 Fifth Avenue
New York, NY 10128–0112
(212) 423-3500
www.guggenheim.org
Works by many Abstract Expressionists including Kline, Motherwell, Pollock, Reinhardt, and Still are on display.

## National Gallery of Art
Sixth Street and Constitution Avenue
Washington, D.C. 20565
(202) 737-4215
www.nga.gov
Work by Abstract Expressionists such as Frankenthaler, Gorky, and Still is exhibited here.

## Albright-Knox Art Gallery
1285 Elmwood Avenue
Buffalo, NY 14222
(716) 882-8700
www.albrightknox.org
Much of Clyfford Still's work is held here.

# Further Reading

## General art books

The *Grove Dictionary of Art* is an excellent general resource. It gives brief definitions of art terms and short biographies of many artists from different backgrounds and schools.

*Abstract Expressionism: The Critical Developments*. Ed. Michael Auping. London and New York: Thames and Hudson, 1987.

*American Abstract Expressionism*. Ed. David Thistlewood. Liverpool, England: Liverpool University Press and Tate Gallery Liverpool, 1993.

Fineberg, Jonathan. *Art Since 1940: Strategies of Being.* Lawrence King Publishing, 2000.

Lucie-Smith, Edward. *Lives of the Great 20th-Century Artists*. London and New York: Thames and Hudson, 1999.

Lawson, Susannah, *The 20th-Century Art Book*. Phaidon Press, 1996.

Gaff, Jackie. *20th Century Art: 1940–1960 Art in Emotion*. Chicago: Heinemann Library, 2000.

## Books about Abstract Expressionist artists

De Kooning, Elaine. *Spirit of Abstract Expressionism*. London: George Braziller, 1994.

Morris, Catherine. *The Essential Willem de Kooning*. New York: Harry N. Abrams Inc., 1999.

Hobbs, Robert. *Lee Krasner.* New York: Abbeville Press, 1993.

Solomon, Deborah. *Jackson Pollock. A Biography*. New York: Simon and Schuster, 1987.

Ratcliff, Carter. *The Fate of a Gesture: Jackson Pollock and Postwar American Art*. New York: Straus and Giroux, 1996.

Ashton, Dore. *About Rothko*. Oxford, England: Oxford University Press, 1983.

# Index